DASH Diet Recipes
Jumpstart Cookbook

**Over 30 Mouthwatering Recipes Ready In 30 Minutes
(Breakfast, Lunch, Dinner, Snack & Dessert Recipes Included!)**

DIANA DAVIS

© 2013 by Diana Davis

All rights reserved. No part of this guide may be reproduced in any form without permission in writing from the publisher except in the case of brief quotations embodied in critical articles or reviews.

Legal & Disclaimer

The information contained in this book is not designed to replace or take the place of any form of medicine or professional medical advice. The information in this book has been provided for educational and entertainment purposes only.

The information contained in this book has been compiled from sources deemed reliable and it is accurate to the best of the Author's knowledge; however, the Author cannot guarantee its accuracy and validity and cannot be held liable for any errors or omissions. Changes are periodically made to this book. You must consult your doctor or get professional medical advice before using any of the suggested remedies, techniques or information in this book.

Upon using the information contained in this book, you agree to hold harmless the Author from and against any damages, costs and expenses, including any legal fees, potentially resulting from the application of any of the information provided by this guide. This disclaimer applies to any damages or injury caused by the use and application, whether directly or indirectly, of any advice or information presented, whether for breach of contract, tort, negligence, personal injury, criminal intent or under any other cause of action.

You agree to accept all risk of using the information presented inside this book. You need to consult a professional medical practitioner in order to ensure you are both able & healthy enough to participate in this program.

PROOF:
Amazon's #1 Best Selling DASH Diet Book

Table of Contents

Acknowledgements 6

Introduction to the Incredible & Proven DASH Diet 7

    How I Stumbled Across the DASH Diet 7

    My Life Then Took A Complete 180-Degree Turn…
    For The Better 8

Over 30 Mouthwatering Recipes Ready In 30 Minutes 11

    Breakfast Recipes 12

        Apple-Spice Baked Oatmeal 12
        Banana-Nut Pancakes 13
        Cheese and Broccoli Mini Egg Omelets 14
        French Toast with Applesauce 15
        Blast-Off Berry Yogurt 16
        Good Morning Quinoa 17
        Mushroom and Shallot Frittata 18

    Lunch Recipes 19

        Apple-Swiss Panini 19
        California Grilled Veggie Sandwich 20
        Tuna Melt Sandwich 21
        Mayo-less Tuna Salad 22
        Turkey, Pear, and Cheese Sandwich 23
        Pizza in a Pita 24
        Salmon Salad Pita 25

Over 30 Mouthwatering Recipes Ready In 30 Minutes

Dinner Recipes 26
   Chicken and Broccoli Stir-Fry 26
   Beef Kebabs with Pineapple Salsa 27
   Brown Rice Burgers 28
   Wild Rice and Chicken Stuffed Tomatoes 29
   Butternut Squash and Chili Pan-Fry 30
   Cilantro-Lime Tilapia Tacos 31
   Cowboy Salad 32

Mouthwatering DASH Diet Snack Recipes 33
   Apple Oat-Bran Muffins 33
   Bean Dip Athenos 34
   Summer Melon Cooler 35
   Pick-Me-Up Lemon Smoothie 35
   Raspberry and Peach Lassi 36
   Lactose-Free Chocolate Pudding 37

Tasty DASH Diet Dessert Recipes 38
   Basmati Rice Pudding with Oranges 38
   Blackberry Oat Nut Crumble 39
   Apple Cranberry Dessert Risotto 40
   Carrot Cake Cookies 41
   Lactose-Free Chocolate Pudding 42

Want To Accelerate Your DASH Diet Results? 43

Check Out Other Books 44

Acknowledgements

Health is the greatest gift, and the second greatest gift is the unconditional care and love from my wonderful family. This includes my loving husband Derek, and my two sons – Matt and Ron. Without them I would not have survived my acute heart failure, much less have the courage to push through my journey to regain my health and write this guide. I am blessed and grateful.

I am indebted to my cousin Deborah who encouraged me to inspire others with my story by sharing my knowledge with the rest of the world. I also want to express my gratitude to my family and friends who, over the past few years, provided their honest feedback to help me refine the processes I share in this guide. Lastly, but most importantly, I want to say a big "THANK YOU" to my readers – yes, that's you! – for giving me an opportunity to help impact their lives. I am both humbled and honored by this.

Introduction to the Incredible & Proven DASH Diet

No, the DASH (Dietary Approaches to Stop Hypertension) Diet is <u>NOT</u> just another health fad.

In 2014, this diet was selected by the US News & World Report as the best and healthiest diet for the <u>4th year in a row</u>. And it is highly recommended by the American Heart Association and the American College of Cardiology as well.

Why? Simply because **it WORKS**.

Research by the foremost National Institutes of Health (NIH) has shown that this incredible diet:

1. Reduces blood pressure & cholesterol
2. Helps us lose weight naturally and without counting calories
3. Reverses or slows down serious illnesses including heart disease, diabetes, and osteoporosis
4. Lowers the risk of developing several different types of cancer…all without involving any medication.

It's no wonder why millions of people from around the world – including myself – now swear by the DASH Diet.

How I Stumbled Across the DASH Diet

Four years ago I found my health spiralling out of control. I was grossly overweight by 70 pounds, and one night I almost died in my sleep from acute heart failure. All I could remember was feeling an intense pain in my chest as if someone was holding my heart and squeezing it with all their might. The pain continued for what felt like an entire lifetime, and the next thing I knew, I was waking up in the hospital.

Fortunately, my struggle for life woke my husband up, and he called for an ambulance that arrived within minutes.

Needless to say, it was a traumatic experience for my entire family, but especially so for my two precious sons – one was five years old, and the other one was seven at the time. When I finally regained consciousness in the hospital, I could see my worried husband and sons, and all of them had tears welling up in their eyes. I can still remember how my heart sank when my sons wrapped their arms around me and asked, "Mommy, are you going to die?"

At that split moment, I decided I never wanted my family to go through the same experience again. I knew it's finally time to take back control of my own health – no matter the price. So I started looking for a diet that could help reduce my weight (my goal was to lose that excess 70 pounds) while reducing the risk of a second heart attack at the same time.

And from the recommendation of a friend, I stumbled upon the DASH Diet.

However, that wasn't the end of the journey. No – it was only the beginning…

Like many other things, there are many books on dieting and contradictory advice between them. I soon realized that the more I read, the more confused I became. But similar to most people, I don't have all the time in the world to read a bunch of those books out there on dieting, and time was even more precious because I could have another heart attack any time.

So out of desperation, I decided to take the "trial and error" approach by putting my health on the line to become my own "lab rat".

My Life Then Took A Complete 180-Degree Turn… For The Better

In just 2 weeks, the results were in:

1. My blood pressure dropped from a risky 150/93 down to the healthy range of 100/71.
2. I lost 10 pounds.

Over 30 Mouthwatering Recipes Ready In 30 Minutes

A year later, my blood pressure had remained in the healthy range, and I had lost a total of 40 pounds. To date currently, I'm happy to report that I've lost over 74 pounds...and counting.

Since then I've been sharing my personal experience and notes about the DASH Diet with my relatives and friends – even before *Mayo Clinic* picked up on the diet.

One of the people I shared my success with was my 33-year-old female cousin – a journalist working in a reputable newspaper firm here in the United States.

After following my suggestions, she lost a little over 10 pounds in just 2½ weeks. She was also the one who came up with the idea for me to write books in order to share my knowledge with the rest of the world, so that's why and when this cookbook was created.

Over 30 Mouthwatering Recipes Ready In 30 Minutes

Inside this cookbook, you'll get **over 30 of the tastiest DASH Diet recipes you can easily prepare and be enjoying in 30 minutes from now**. These are just some of out of the 80 recipes I share in my complete *DASH Diet Recipes Complete Cookbook* here: http://amzn.to/1k95lhR

All of the recipes come with additional information like sodium level and calories (there's no need to track calories in this diet though) in case you want to track them.

Finally, you can now kiss goodbye to spending hours in the kitchen!

Ready? Let's get started!

Breakfast Recipes

Apple-Spice Baked Oatmeal

Oatmeal is a great staple in the DASH Diet because of its many health benefits. To ramp up a boring oatmeal recipe, try this baked version that has a kick from your favorite fruit. You can swap out the apple with bananas, blueberries, or pear.

Preparation Time: 30 minutes

Servings: 9

Ingredients:

- 1 egg, beaten
- ½ c. sweetened applesauce
- ½ c. non-fat or 1% milk
- 1 tsp. vanilla
- 2 T. oil
- 1 apple, chopped
- 2 c. rolled oats
- 1 tsp. baking powder
- ¼ tsp. salt
- 1 tsp. cinnamon
- 2 T. brown sugar
- 2 T. chopped nuts

Instructions:

1. Preheat an oven to 375° F. Lightly oil an 8 x 8-inch baking pan.
2. Mix applesauce, egg, milk, vanilla, and oil in a bowl then add in the apple. In another bowl, combine baking powder, rolled oats, cinnamon, and salt, and add this to the liquid mixture and mix well. Pour the mixture into the prepared baking dish and bake for about 25 minutes.
3. Remove from the oven when done and sprinkle with brown sugar and nuts. Allow to broil in the oven for an additional 3-4 minutes until the top is brown and sugar bubbles start to appear.
4. Cut into squares and serve warm.

Additional Nutritional Information:

Calories: 160 per serving

Sodium: 150 mg.

Over 30 Mouthwatering Recipes Ready In 30 Minutes

Banana-Nut Pancakes

Pancakes are a delicious breakfast staple. This version will jazz up your morning with a much-needed protein boost. To further amp it up, try topping the pancakes with non-fat vanilla yogurt instead of syrup.

Preparation Time: 20 minutes

Servings: 6

Ingredients:

- 1 c. whole-wheat flour
- 2 tsp. baking powder
- ¼ tsp. salt
- ¼ tsp. cinnamon
- 1 large banana, mashed
- 1 c. 1% milk
- 3 large egg whites
- 2 tsp. oil
- 1 tsp. vanilla
- 2 T. walnuts, chopped

Instructions:

1. Mix all dry ingredients together in a large bowl.
2. In a different bowl, mix oil, milk, egg whites, mashed bananas, and vanilla until smooth.
3. Combine the wet ingredients with the dry, but DO NOT over mix.
4. Heat a large skillet over medium heat and lightly spray with cooking oil. Pour around ¼ cup of the pancake batter on the hot skillet. When the batter starts to set and bubble, flip it over. Repeat with the remaining batter.

Additional Nutritional Information:

Calories: 146 per serving

Sodium: 331 mg.

Cheese and Broccoli Mini Egg Omelets

This classy dish will make you feel like breakfast-in-bed royalty. You can pair this omelet with a fruit salad, low-fat milk, or whole-wheat toast in order to enjoy a complete and well-balanced diet.

Preparation Time: 30 minutes

Servings: 9

Ingredients:

- 2 c. broccoli florets
- 4 eggs
- 1 c. egg whites
- ¼ c. reduced-fat cheddar cheese
- ¼ c. grated Romano or parmesan cheese
- 1 T. olive oil
- salt and pepper to taste
- Cooking spray

Instructions:

1. Preheat oven to 350° F.

2. In a small saucepan, steam broccoli with water for about 6-7 minutes.

3. Once broccoli is cooked, drain well then mash with salt, pepper, and oil.

4. Spray a muffin tin lightly with cooking oil then spoon broccoli evenly into each muffin well.

5. In a separate bowl, beat egg whites, grated parmesan cheese, eggs, salt, and pepper. Pour this mixture into the spooned broccoli mixture in the muffin pan. Top with grated cheddar and bake for 20 minutes. Serve immediately.

Additional Nutritional Information:

Calories: 104 per serving (1 mini-omelet)

Sodium: 213 mg.

Over 30 Mouthwatering Recipes Ready In 30 Minutes

French Toast with Applesauce

French toast is a favorite way to improve up your mornings. In order to give it a healthier edge, you can use 4 egg whites instead of 2 eggs for the batter, mix it with cinnamon or nutmeg, or pair it with a glass of milk for extra nutrition.

Preparation time: 10 minutes

Servings: 6

Ingredients:

- 2 eggs
- ½ c. milk
- ½ tsp. ground cinnamon
- 2 T. white sugar
- ¼ c. unsweetened applesauce
- 6 slices whole-wheat bread

Instructions:

1. Combine eggs, milk, sugar, cinnamon, and applesauce in a mixing bowl.
2. Wet each piece of bread with the mixture allowing the excess to drip off before placing in a lightly greased skillet.
3. Cook each side of the bread until it is golden brown in color. Serve hot.

Additional Nutritional Information:

Calories per Servings: 150

Sodium: 220 mg.

Blast-Off Berry Yogurt

Yogurt is a great food to enjoy on the DASH Diet. This parfait can provide extra energy for the day with the addition of fruit and nuts.

Preparation Time: 5 minutes

Servings: 4

Ingredients:

- 1 c. strawberries
- 1 c. low-fat granola
- 1 c. blueberries
- 1 c. plain, low-fat yogurt

Instructions:

1. Divide strawberries evenly between the 4 glasses, and sprinkle granola over the strawberries in each glass.
2. Divide blueberries into each glass as well.
3. Spoon yogurt on top of the blueberries in each glass and serve.

Additional Nutritional Information:

Calories per Servings: 150

Sodium: 85 mg.

Good Morning Quinoa

Gluten-free and a great source of calcium and protein – this is a perfect one-dish DASH breakfast!

Preparation Time: 30 minutes

Servings: 4

Ingredients:

- 2 c. low-fat on non-fat milk
- 1 c. uncooked quinoa
- ¼ c. honey or brown sugar
- ¼ tsp. cinnamon
- ¼ c. sliced or slivered almonds
- ¼ c. dried currants, dried apricots, or fresh berries

Instructions:

1. Rinse quinoa thoroughly.
2. In a medium saucepan, bring milk to a boil.
3. Add the quinoa and bring back to a boil.
4. Cover then reduce heat to low and simmer for 12-15 minutes until most of the liquid is absorbed.
5. Remove from heat and fluff with fork.
6. Stir the rest of the ingredients, cover, and allow to stand for 15 minutes.

Additional Nutritional Information:

Calories per Servings: 320

Sodium: 70 mg.

Mushroom and Shallot Frittata

For a well-balanced and nutrient-rich meal, serve this with fresh fruit, whole grain bread, and a glass of milk. The savory veggies and sharp parmesan cheese make for a tasty combination in this egg-based dish.

Preparation Time: 30 minutes

Servings: 4

Ingredients:

- 1 T. unsalted butter
- 4 shallots, finely chopped
- ½ lb. mushrooms
- 2 T. fresh parsley, finely chopped
- 1 tsp. dried thyme
- 3 eggs
- black pepper to taste
- 5 large egg whites
- 1 T. milk or fat-free half-and-half
- ¼ c. fresh-grated parmesan cheese

Instructions:

1. Preheat oven to 350° F.
2. On the stovetop, melt butter in a large, oven-safe skillet. Stir in shallots and sauté until golden brown.
3. Add parsley, thyme, mushrooms, and black pepper.
4. In another bowl, whisk eggs and egg whites together with parmesan cheese and milk.
5. Add the egg mixture to the skillet.
6. When the edges begin to set, place the entire skillet in the oven.
7. Bake until frittata is fully cooked, about 15 minutes.
8. Cut into four wedges and serve.

Additional Nutritional Information:

Calories per Servings: 160 per wedge

Sodium: 250 mg.

Over 30 Mouthwatering Recipes Ready In 30 Minutes

Lunch Recipes

Apple-Swiss Panini

You can substitute reduced-fat cheddar cheese for the Swiss cheese if preferred. If you don't happen to have arugula on hand, you can use leaf lettuce or fresh spinach. This also pairs well with a glass of fat-free milk.

Preparation Time: 10 minutes

Servings: 4

Ingredients:

- 8 slices whole-grain bread
- ¼ c. non-fat honey mustard
- 2 apples, thinly sliced
- 6 oz. low-fat Swiss cheese
- 1 c. arugula leaves

Instructions:

1. Preheat your Panini press or a non-stick skillet if you don't have a press.
2. Lightly spread honey mustard on each slice of bread.
3. Layer arugula, apple slices, and cheese then top with remaining bread slices.
4. Grill each sandwich for 3-5 minutes or until cheese has melted and bread is toasted.
5. Remove from pan and allow to cool slightly.

Additional Nutritional Information:

Calories per Servings: 280
Sodium: 480 mg.

California Grilled Veggie Sandwich

You can enjoy this sandwich with a side of low-fat yogurt topped with frozen berries to provide even more DASH variations.

Preparation Time: 10 minutes

Servings: 4

Ingredients:

- 3 T. light mayonnaise
- 3 cloves garlic
- 1 T. lemon juice
- 1/8 c. olive oil
- 1 c. red bell peppers
- 1 small zucchini
- 1 red onion
- 1 small yellow squash
- 2 slices focaccia bread
- ½ c. reduced-fat feta cheese

Instructions:

1. Mix mayonnaise, minced garlic, and lemon juice in a bowl then set aside in the refrigerator.
2. Preheat grill on high heat.
3. Brush vegetables with olive oil on each side then place them on the lightly oiled grill pan.
4. Cook for about 3 minutes.
5. Spread some of the mayonnaise mixture on the insides of the bread and sprinkle with feta cheese.
6. Place on the grill, cheese sides on the inside, and close the lid for 2-3 minutes while it cooks.
7. Remove sandwich from the grill and layer with vegetables then serve.

Additional Nutritional Information:

Calories per Servings: 240

Sodium: 490 mg.

Over 30 Mouthwatering Recipes Ready In 30 Minutes

Tuna Melt Sandwich

This pairs easily with an apple and a side salad, and Viola! Lunch is served!

Preparation Time: 10 minutes

Servings: 4

Ingredients:

- 6 oz. white tuna packed in water
- 1/3 c. celery, chopped
- ¼ c. onion, chopped
- ¼ c. low-fat Russian or Thousand Island dressing
- 2 whole-wheat English muffins
- 3 slices cheddar cheese
- salt and black pepper

Instructions:

1. Preheat broiler.
2. Combine tuna, onion, celery, and salad dressing then season to taste with salt and pepper.
3. Split English muffins in half and toast then top the split-side up with ¼ of the tuna mixture.
4. Broil 2-3 minutes or until heated through.
5. Top with cheese and return to broiler until the cheese is melted.

Additional Nutritional Information:

Calories per Servings: 210

Sodium: 417 mg.

Mayo-less Tuna Salad

If you prefer, you can substitute spring greens for the arugula. You also want to try to choose tuna that has less than 200 mg. per serving according to the label. Serve with a cup of low-sodium soup or a piece of fruit and milk for a well-balanced diet.

Preparation Time: 5 minutes

Servings: 2

Ingredients:

- 5 oz. light tuna in water
- 1 T. extra virgin olive oil
- 1 T. red wine vinegar
- ¼ c. green onion, chopped
- 2 c. arugula
- 1 c. cooked pasta
- 1 T. fresh shaved parmesan cheese
- black pepper to taste

Instructions:

In a large bowl, toss the tuna with vinegar, oil, onion, arugula, and cooked pasta. Divide between two plates and top with parmesan cheese and black pepper.

Additional Nutritional Information:

Calories per Servings: 245

Sodium: 290 mg.

Turkey, Pear, and Cheese Sandwich

When making this sandwich, be careful about the sodium content. Shop for lean deli meats and pair the sandwich with fruits and veggies for a well-balanced DASH Diet meal.

Preparation Time: 10 minutes

Servings: 2

Ingredients:

- 2 slices multi-grain or rye bread
- 2 tsp. Dijon-style mustard
- 2 slices reduced-sodium cooked or smoked turkey
- 1 pear
- ¼ c. low-fat mozzarella cheese

Instructions:

1. Spread each side of the bread with teaspoon of mustard.
2. Place one slice turkey on each side of the bread. Arrange pear slices on top of the turkey the sprinkle with two tablespoons of cheese each.
3. Broil until the turkey is warm and cheese is completely melted.
4. Cut each sandwich slice in half and serve open-faced.

Additional Nutritional Information:

Calories per Servings: 190

Sodium: 480 mg.

Pizza in a Pita

Try to pair this meal with fresh salad greens and top with walnuts, pears, and light vinaigrette.

Preparation Time: 10 minutes

Servings: 2

Ingredients:

- 2 whole-wheat pita breads
- ½ c. reduced-sodium mozzarella cheese
- ¼ c. pizza, spaghetti, or tomato sauce
- Veggies of choice include mushrooms, bell peppers, olives, onions, and/or artichoke hearts.

Instructions:

1. Preheat oven to 350° F.
2. Split bread halfway through the edge in order to stuff with the cheese, tomato sauce, and any other preferred toppings.
3. Wrap the pita bread and its fillings in aluminum foil and bake until the cheese melts.

Additional Nutritional Information:

Calories per Servings: 170

Sodium: 300 mg.

Over 30 Mouthwatering Recipes Ready In 30 Minutes

Salmon Salad Pita

This healthy lunch is super heart-friendly with its omega-3 content. As a healthy substitute for tartar sauce, you can also use plain fat-free yogurt and lemon wedges. You can use also use crackers instead of pita bread if preferred.

Preparation Time: 5 minutes

Servings: 3

Ingredients:

- ¾ c. canned Alaska Salmon
- 3 T. plain fat-free yogurt
- 1 T. lemon juice
- 2 T. red bell pepper
- 1 T. red onion
- 1 tsp. caper
- 3 lettuce leaves
- 3 small whole-wheat pita breads
- a pinch of dill
- fresh black pepper to taste

Instructions:

1. Mix the first eight ingredients in a bowl and combine well.
2. Place one lettuce leaf and 1/3 salmon spread in each pita bread.
3. Serve immediately.

Additional Nutritional Information:

Calories per Servings: 180

Sodium: 331 mg.

Dinner Recipes

Chicken and Broccoli Stir-Fry

In order to limit sugar content, use 100% orange juice and most nutrients from your meals! Enjoy a glass of nutrient-rich, low-fat or non-fat milk to round out the recipe.

Preparation Time: 30 minutes

Servings: 4

Ingredients:

- 1/3 c. orange juice
- 1 T. low-sodium soy sauce
- 1 T. Schezuan sauce
- 2 tsp. cornstarch
- 1 T. canola oil
- 1 lb. boneless chicken breast
- 2 c. frozen broccoli florets
- 1 (6-oz.) pack frozen snow peas
- 2 c. shredded cabbage
- 2 c. cooked brown rice
- 1 T. sesame seeds

Instructions:

1. Mix orange juice, Schezuan sauce, soy sauce, and cornstarch in a small bowl and set aside.
2. Heat oil in a wok, add chicken, and lightly cook.
3. Add cabbage, broccoli, sauce mixture, and snow peas to the chicken and continue to cook for around five minutes until vegetables are heated through and the chicken is completely cooked.
4. Sprinkle with sesame seeds, and serve over brown rice.

Additional Nutritional Information:

Calories per Servings: 340

Sodium: 240 mg.

Beef Kebabs with Pineapple Salsa

Grilling is a terrific way of enhancing the natural flavors in food without additional salt. This slow grilling helps caramelize flavors in order to give a sweet smokiness to the flavor that's quite appealing to your tastebuds.

Preparation Time: 30 minutes

Servings: 6

Ingredients:

- 2 T. lime juice
- 2 T. olive oil
- 2 cloves garlic
- 1 jalapeno pepper
- ½ tsp. ground cumin
- ½ medium pineapple
- 1 red onion
- 1 green bell pepper
- 2 tsp. freshly grated lime peel
- ½ tsp. salt
- beefsteaks

Instructions:

1. Cut beefsteaks into cubes.
2. Combine first five ingredients to make the marinade making sure to reserve about two tablespoons to use for the salsa.
3. Place the beef into the marinade and toss to coat well.
4. Thread beef cubes onto the skewers and alternatively thread with the fruits and veggies.
5. Place each kebab on a hot grill until meat is cooked and everything is seared nicely.
6. Serve with the pineapple salsa.

Additional Nutritional Information:

Calories per Servings: 207

Sodium: 259 mg.

DASH Diet Recipes Jumpstart Cookbook

Brown Rice Burgers

These meatless burgers taste just as good as the real thing. Pair them with a whole-wheat bun, tomatoes, and lettuce, and you're good to go! Try with a side of grilled asparagus for complete and healthier DASH option.

Preparation Time: 10 minutes

Servings: 12

Ingredients:

- 2 c. cooked brown rice
- ½ c. parsley
- 1 carrot, chopped
- ½ c. onion
- 1 clove garlic
- 2 eggs, beaten
- ½ c. whole-wheat flour
- 2 T. vegetable oil
- 1 tsp. salt
- ½ tsp. ground black pepper

Instructions:

1. In a mixing bowl, combine all ingredients except for the oil.
2. Form into patties.
3. Heat and lightly grease a grill pan or skillet and cook each burger patty through.
4. Serve with a bun and vegetables.

Additional Nutritional Information:

Calories per Servings: 120

Sodium: 150 mg.

Wild Rice and Chicken Stuffed Tomatoes

These ripe tomatoes are stuffed with wild rice, savory chicken, parmesan cheese, and basil. Serve these tomatoes warm with toasted whole-wheat artisan bread for a filling DASH meal.

Preparation Time: 30 minutes

Servings: 4

Ingredients:

- 1 c. uncooked wild rice
- 1 c. low-sodium vegetable broth
- 1 c. water
- 1 chicken breast
- 4 large red tomatoes
- 2 T. fresh basil
- 2 cloves garlic
- ½ c. shredded parmesan cheese
- 2 T. olive oil

Instructions:

1. Cook the wild rice according to package directions using the vegetable broth and water to cook it.
2. Preheat oven to 350° F. Grill the chicken breast then slice into ½-inch thick pieces.
3. Cut off the top of each tomato and scoop out the fleshy interior.
4. Once the rice is cooked, mix with the chicken, basil, garlic, and parmesan cheese.
5. Stuff the tomatoes with wild rice and sprinkle with parmesan cheese.
6. Brush with oil and bake in the oven for 10 minutes.

Additional Nutritional Information:

Calories per Servings: 250

Sodium: 230 mg.

DASH Diet Recipes Jumpstart Cookbook

Butternut Squash and Chili Pan-Fry

This is a good source of Vitamin A which is known for keeping eyes and skin healthy. That definitely makes this a perfect DASH recipe to try!

Preparation Time: 30 minutes

Servings: 10

Ingredients:

- 1 medium butternut squash
- 1 lb. fresh green Poblano chilies
- 1½ T. olive or vegetable oil
- 1 medium onion
- ½ tsp. chili powder
- 1 c. grated cheese
- 1 tsp. salt

Instructions:

1. Peel squash, cut in half, remove the seeds, and cut into ½-inch pieces.
2. Prepare the chilies by roasting them over a stovetop flame than allow to cool.
3. Heat oil over medium heat then add onions and cook while stirring for three minutes.
4. Add squash, chili powder, and salt.
5. Cover and cook for an additional minute or so then add in the chilies and cook for another three minutes.
6. Sprinkle with cheese and cover again until the cheese melts.
7. Serve hot.

Additional Nutritional Information:

Calories per Servings: 60

Sodium: 3 mg.

Cilantro-Lime Tilapia Tacos

This is fresh and light meal is perfect for a warm summer's night. To liven the meal up, add cilantro and lime juice plus jalapeno for a kick of flavor.

Preparation Time: 20 minutes

Servings: 4

Ingredients:

- 1 lb. Tilapia fillets
- 1 tsp. olive oil
- 1 small onion
- 4 cloves garlic
- 2 jalapeno peppers
- 2 c. diced tomatoes
- ¼ c. fresh cilantro
- 8 white corn tortilla
- 1 c. shredded cabbage
- 4 T. low-fat sour cream
- juice of 3 limes
- lime wedges and cilantro for garnish

Instructions:

1. Heat olive oil in a skillet and sauté onions until translucent then add garlic.
2. Place tilapia in the skillet and cook until flesh starts to flake.
3. Add jalapeno peppers, cilantro, tomatoes, and lime juice.
4. Sauté over medium high-heat and mix well.
5. Heat tortillas to keep warm.
6. Scoop about ¼ cup of the fish onto the tortilla followed by shredded cabbage and sour cream.
7. Serve with cilantro and lime wedges.

Additional Nutritional Information:

Calories per Servings: 427

Sodium: 142 mg.

Cowboy Salad

Use this great salad as a side for grilled barbecue, as a dip, or as a great topping for any lean meat dish.

Preparation Time: 10 minutes

Servings: 12

Ingredients:

- 2 cans black beans
- 1 can corn
- 1 small bunch cilantro
- 1 bunch green onions
- 3 medium tomatoes
- 1 avocado
- 1 T. canola or vegetable oil
- 2 T. vinegar
- lime juice, salt, and pepper to taste

Instructions:

1. Drain and rinse the corn and black beans in a colander.
2. Finely chop cilantro and onions, dice avocados and tomatoes, and mix all together with drained corn and beans in a large bowl until well-combined.
3. Mix oil, vinegar, salt, and pepper in a small bowl. Drizzle over the salad mix and toss well to coat evenly.
4. Serve as a meal with your favorite tortilla chips.

Additional Nutritional Information:

Calories per Servings: 70

Sodium: 150 mg.

Over 30 Mouthwatering Recipes Ready In 30 Minutes

Mouthwatering DASH Diet Snack Recipes

Apple Oat-Bran Muffins

These muffins are much healthier than store-bought baked goods and even more tasty. In addition, they are low in cholesterol and saturated fat. Bake up a bunch of these to store in the freezer for a quick snack or even breakfast.

Preparation Time: 25 minutes

Servings: 12

Ingredients:

- ¾ c. all-purpose flour
- ¾ c. whole-wheat flour
- 1½ tsp. cinnamon
- 1 tsp. baking powder
- ½ tsp. baking soda
- ¼ tsp. salt
- 1 c. buttermilk
- ½ c. oat bran
- ¼ c. brown sugar
- 2 T. vegetable oil
- 1 large egg
- 1½ c. apples, chopped

Instructions:

1. Preheat oven to 400° F.
2. Lightly grease a muffin pan or line with cupcake papers.
3. Combine both kinds of flour, cinnamon, baking powder, baking soda, and salt in a large mixing bowl.
4. In a medium bowl, beat together buttermilk, oat bran, oil, brown sugar, and egg until blended.
5. Stir buttermilk mixture into flour mixture just until combined then fold in apples.
6. Divide batter among muffin cups, and bake for 18-20 minutes until a toothpick inserted in the middle comes out clean.
7. Cool muffins in the pan for five minutes (if not using liners) then remove from pan and cool on a wire rack.

Additional Nutritional Information:

Calories per Servings: 121
Sodium: 134 mg.

Bean Dip Athenos

The DASH Diet utilizes many servings of beans, nuts, and seeds for optimal nutrition and healthy eating. In order to follow the guidelines, pair this dip with vegetables or crackers or simply spread on sandwiches for a tasty snack or even a light meal.

Preparation Time: 5 minutes

Servings: 24

Ingredients:

- 3½ c. garbanzo or navy beans
- 2/3 c. fat-free sour cream
- 2 tsp. garlic, minced
- 4 T. balsamic vinegar
- ¼ c. chopped, sun-dried tomatoes
- ¼ c. parsley
- 2 T. Kalamata or chopped olives

Instructions:

1. Place all ingredients in a blender and combine to a smooth paste.
2. Serve with veggies and crackers.

Additional Nutritional Information:

Calories per Servings: 54 per 2 tablespoons

Sodium: 100 mg.

Summer Melon Cooler

For the best taste, allow this beverage to chill thoroughly before drinking. It is a good source of vitamin C which helps prevent bleeding gums and keeps blood vessels healthy.

Preparation Time: two minutes

Servings: 3

Ingredients:

- 2 c. cantaloupe
- 1 c. low-fat lemon yogurt
- 1 c. orange juice

Instructions:

Blend all ingredients until smooth and chill before serving.

Additional Nutritional Information:

Calories per Servings: 120

Sodium: 75 mg.

Pick-Me-Up Lemon Smoothie

Try this tangy smoothie after a workout and enjoy feeling the refreshment it provides! You can also create a simple but healthy breakfast by adding a handful of almonds or an apple oat-bran muffin.

Preparation Time: two minutes

Servings: 1

Ingredients:

- 3 milk ice cubes
- 1 container of plain, fat-free yogurt

- 2 T. granulated sugar
- 1 tsp. lemon juice
- ½ tsp. grated lemon zest

Instructions:

Blend all ingredients until smooth and serve once chilled.

Additional Nutritional Information:

Calories per Servings: 190

Sodium: 167 mg.

Raspberry and Peach Lassi

Enjoy much-needed refreshment on a hot summer evening with this cool drink. A traditional Indian recipe, this lassi is sure to meet your dessert cravings as well.

Preparation Time: two minutes

Servings: 2

Ingredients:

- 1 c. peaches
- ½ medium ripe banana
- ½ c. raspberries
- 1 c. low-fat buttermilk
- 2-3 ice cubes

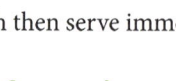

Instructions:

Blend all ingredients until smooth then serve immediately.

Additional Nutritional Information:

Calories per Servings: 120

Sodium: 130 mg.

Lactose-Free Chocolate Pudding

This pudding absolutely fits the DASH guidelines, and can be layered with fruit to make a yummy parfait.

Preparation Time: 30 minutes

Servings: 8

Ingredients:

- 4 c. low-fat lactose-free milk
- ¼ c. cornstarch
- ¼ c. unsweetened cocoa powder
- ¼ tsp. kosher salt
- 2 oz. unsweetened chocolate
- ¼ c. plus 2 T. sugar
- 1 tsp. pure vanilla extract

Instructions:

1. Blend half of the milk and cornstarch in a small bowl.
2. Combine salt and cocoa powder in a saucepan over medium heat. Slowly whisk in the remaining milk, chocolate, and sugar while heating until chocolate has melted.
3. Whisk in the cornstarch mixture and cook until very thick and just beginning to boil.
4. Remove from heat and stir in the vanilla extract.
5. Allow to cool slightly while stirring occasionally to keep it warm throughout.
6. Pour pudding into individual custard dishes or small bowls.

Additional Nutritional Information:

Calories per Servings: 162

Sodium: 123 mg.

Tasty DASH Diet Dessert Recipes

Basmati Rice Pudding with Oranges

Here's a great tip – in order to get the seeds out of the pomegranate easily, cut it in half and put the cut side face down on a hard surface then whack the bottom with a spoon or spatula in order to release the seeds.

Preparation Time: 30 minutes

Servings: 6

Ingredients:

- ¾ c. basmati rice
- 3 navel oranges
- ½ vanilla bean
- 4 c. fat-free evaporated milk
- ¼ c. low-fat sweet condensed milk
- 4 T. sugar
- 2 T. pistachios
- 2 T. pomegranate seeds

Instructions:

1. In a saucepan, boil two cups of water, add rice, and cook until done.
2. Wash one of the oranges and remove one teaspoon of zest from the rind taking care to reserve the juice from that orange.
3. Cut off the rind (or peel) of the remaining oranges and remove the pits then cut into segments.
4. When rice is tender, add orange juice and zest, evaporated and condensed milks, vanilla bean, and sugar.
5. Cook over medium heat until creamy in consistency.
6. Remove the vanilla bean and divide the mixture evenly among individual bowls and serve warm.

Additional Nutritional Information:

Calories per Servings: 286

Sodium: 210 mg.

Over 30 Mouthwatering Recipes Ready In 30 Minutes

Blackberry Oat Nut Crumble

Enjoy summer berries in the winter with this winning DASH Diet recipe. Add a scoop of vanilla ice cream over the hot crumble and let your taste buds party!

Preparation Time: 30 minutes

Servings: 4

Ingredients:

- 2 T. sugar
- 1 T. cornstarch
- 2 c. blackberries
- ½ tsp. lemon juice
- ½ c. rolled oats
- ¼ c. all-purpose flour
- ¼ c. brown sugar
- ½ tsp. cinnamon
- 1/8 tsp. salt
- 1 T. unsalted butter
- ¼ c. hazelnuts

Instructions:

1. Preheat oven to 350° F. Use a non-stick spray to coat an 8 x 8-inch baking pan.
2. Combine cornstarch and sugar in a mixing bowl. Add the berries and lemon juice and stir to combine. Pour berries into a prepared baking dish making sure to scrape out any sugar and starch from the bowl.
3. Combine oats, flour, brown sugar, salt, and cinnamon in another bowl.
4. Add in the diced butter and cut the ingredients with a fork or pastry blender. Stir in chopped hazelnuts.
5. Spread the crumble topping over the berries and bake in the oven. Serve warm.

Additional Nutritional Information:

Calories per Servings: 240

Sodium: 75 mg.

Apple Cranberry Dessert Risotto

Risotto has increased in popularity to become one of the hottest Italian food items on the menu. You will especially enjoy a dessert version of this dish. The wine can be replaced with milk and/or water and still be just as enjoyable.

Preparation Time: 30 minutes

Servings: 4

Ingredients:

- ½ c. dried cranberries
- 3½ c. fat-free milk
- 1 cinnamon stick
- 1 T. butter
- 1 apple
- ½ c. arborio rice
- 1½ c. apple cider
- 2 T. light brown sugar
- Pinch of salt

Instructions:

1. Cover dried cranberries with water in a small bowl and set aside to plump.
2. In a saucepan, combine milk, cinnamon, and salt and heat until hot but not boiling. Remove from heat, set aside, and allow to steep.
3. In another saucepan, melt butter then add apple and cook until tender. Add in the rice and continue to cook while stirring frequently until most of the liquid has evaporated. Add sugar and the milk mixture.
4. Continue cooking while adding the liquid until the rice has a creamy consistency.
5. Discard the cinnamon stick.
6. Drain cranberries and stir into the risotto then serve dish warm.

Additional Nutritional Information:

Calories per Servings: 336

Sodium: 103 mg.

Carrot Cake Cookies

Treat your tummy to this low-calorie cookie that's full of protein and fiber. Your sweet tooth will surely be happy and healthy!

Preparation Time: 20 minutes

Servings: 48

Ingredients:

- ½ c. light-brown sugar
- ½ c. sugar
- ½ c. oil
- ½ c. applesauce or fruit puree
- 2 eggs
- 1 tsp. vanilla
- 1 c. flour
- 1 c. whole-wheat flour
- 1 tsp. baking soda
- 1 tsp. baking powder
- ¼ tsp. salt
- 1 tsp. ground cinnamon
- ½ tsp. ground nutmeg
- ½ tsp. ground ginger
- 2 c. old-fashioned rolled oats
- 1½ c. carrots, finely grated
- 1 c. golden raisins

Instructions:

1. Preheat oven to 350° F.
2. Mix oil, sugars, applesauce, eggs, and vanilla thoroughly.
3. Sift dry ingredients together then blend with wet ingredients.
4. Stir in raisins and carrots.
5. Drop by teaspoons-full onto a greased cookie sheet.
6. Bake for 12-15 minutes until golden brown.
7. Store in an airtight container.

Additional Nutritional Information:

Calories per Servings: 80

Sodium: 55 mg.

Lactose-Free Chocolate Pudding

This pudding absolutely fits the DASH guidelines, and can be layered with fruit to make a yummy parfait.

Preparation Time: 30 minutes

Servings: 8

Ingredients:

- 4 c. low-fat lactose-free milk
- ¼ c. cornstarch
- ¼ c. unsweetened cocoa powder
- ¼ tsp. kosher salt
- 2 oz. unsweetened chocolate
- ¼ c. plus 2 T. sugar
- 1 tsp. pure vanilla extract

Instructions:

1. Blend half of the milk and cornstarch in a small bowl.
2. Combine salt and cocoa powder in a saucepan over medium heat. Slowly whisk in the remaining milk, chocolate, and sugar while heating until chocolate has melted.
3. Whisk in the cornstarch mixture and cook until very thick and just beginning to boil.
4. Remove from heat and stir in the vanilla extract.
5. Allow to cool slightly while stirring occasionally to keep it warm throughout.
6. Pour pudding into individual custard dishes or small bowls.

Additional Nutritional Information:

Calories per Servings: 162

Sodium: 123 mg.

Want To Accelerate Your DASH Diet Results?

If you'd like to accelerate your results with the DASH Diet, I invite you to take on my complete *DASH Diet Recipes Complete Cookbook* guide.

In my guide, I'll share with you:

- **The 2 Types of DASH Diet** – and which one you should adopt.
- **The Easy-To-Follow, 5-Step DASH Diet Success Formula** – I don't know about you, but I've never had much success "jumping in the deep end". This book gives you a more realistic approach to gradually bring this wonderful diet into your life so you don't risk shocking your body (literally) with too many changes too soon…
- **What to Eat More of and How Much** – With the help of my summary table, you'll know exactly what foods to eat, when to eat then, and how much which leaves little room for confusion or doubts.
- **50 Additional Mouth-watering DASH Diet Recipes for Breakfast, Lunch, Dinner, & Snacks** – With 80 delicious recipes in total, you'll have a wide variety to choose from, so you won't have to eat the same dish over and over again. In addition, they can be easily prepared in 30 minutes or less. And as an added bonus, young children in my family love them too!
- *And much, much more…*

This guide is a result of my experimenting with the often confusing and contradictory advice dished out by various DASH Diet authors.

It's fun, it's exciting and it's packed with practical steps to accelerate your results with the DASH Diet.

Whenever you feel that you are ready to learn more, you can get your hands on the *DASH Diet Recipes Complete Cookbook* guide or by visiting here: http://amzn.to/1k95lhR

Check Out Other Books

Below you'll find some of the other popular books that are popular on Amazon and Kindle as well. Simply visit their URL below to check them out.

Slow Cooker Recipes Quick & Easy Cookbook - Mouthwatering Recipes Prepared in 30 Minutes or Less!

http://amzn.to/1kaxG9W

High Protein Low Carb Diet - Lose Weight Effortlessly & Permanently

http://amzn.to/1dBDxxu

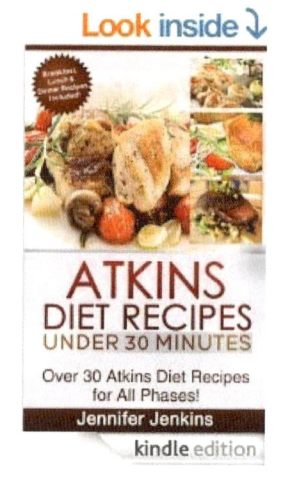

Atkins Diet Recipes Under 30 Minutes - Over 30 Atkins Recipes For All Phases (Includes Atkins Induction Recipes)

http://amzn.to/NyfMA5

Made in the USA
Lexington, KY
29 June 2014